UNLEASHING THE POWER OF MULTIBAGGER STOCKS

A COMPREHENSIVE GUIDE TO IDENTIFYING AND INVESTING IN HIGH-GROWTH COMPANIES

FINANCE POETRY

Made with ♥ on the Notion Press Platform
www.notionpress.com

Contents

Contents

Preface

Investing in the stock market can be a daunting task, especially for those who are new to the game. With so many different companies and stocks to choose from, it can be challenging to know where to start. However, for those who are willing to put in the time and effort, there are opportunities to make significant gains by investing in high-growth companies known as "multibagger stocks."

In this book, we will explore the concept of multibagger investing and provide a comprehensive guide to identifying and investing in these high-growth companies. We will cover the various approaches to identifying multibagger stocks, including fundamental and technical analysis, as well as top-down and bottom-up approaches.

We will also discuss the importance of valuation in multibagger investing, and how to analyse industry trends and market dynamics to find the best opportunities. We will provide strategies for investing in multibagger stocks for long-term success, as well as portfolio management techniques to diversify your investments.

Throughout the book, we will provide case studies of successful Multibagger investments and highlight common mistakes to avoid when investing in these high-growth companies. We will also discuss when to sell your multibagger stocks and take profits.

By the end of this book, readers will have a solid understanding of multibagger investing and the tools and strategies needed to identify and invest in these high-growth companies.

Happy Investing!

CHAPTER ONE

What Are Multibagger Stocks?

Multibagger stocks are stocks that have the potential to grow exponentially and deliver significant returns to investors over the long term. The term "multibagger" is used to describe stocks that have the potential to increase in value by multiple times their current price.

Investors typically look for multibagger stocks because they offer the potential for significant returns that can outpace the broader market. However, investing in multibagger stocks is not without risk. Many of these stocks are relatively unknown companies or industries, and there is often a high degree of uncertainty surrounding their future prospects.

To identify potential multibagger stocks, investors may look for companies that have a unique product or service offering, a strong competitive advantage, and a long-term growth plan. They may also look for companies that operate in industries with high growth potential, such as technology, healthcare, or renewable energy.

It's important to note that not all multibagger stocks will achieve their potential. Some may fail to meet expectations, and others may experience setbacks or challenges along the way. Therefore, it's essential to conduct thorough research and analysis before investing in any stock, particularly those that have the potential for significant returns.

Overall, investing in multibagger stocks can be a high-risk, high-reward strategy. However, by carefully selecting stocks with strong growth potential and maintaining a long-term investment horizon, investors may be able to achieve significant returns over time.

CHAPTER TWO

The Psychology of Investing in Multibagger Stocks

Investing in multibagger stocks is not just about crunching numbers and analysing financial statements. It also involves understanding the psychology of investing and how emotions can impact investment decisions. In this chapter, we will explore the psychology of investing in multibagger stocks and provide strategies for managing emotions to make better investment decisions.

One of the primary emotions that can impact investment decisions is fear. Fear can cause investors to panic and sell their stocks during market downturns, leading to missed opportunities for long-term gains. On the other hand, greed can also be a driving force in investing, causing investors to chase high-risk, high-reward stocks without considering the potential downsides.

To manage these emotions, it is important to have a clear investment strategy in place. This strategy should be based on your risk tolerance, financial goals, and investment timeline. By having a solid plan in place, you can make more rational investment decisions and avoid making impulsive decisions based on emotions.

Another important aspect of managing emotions in investing is to have a long-term perspective. Multibagger stocks are not built overnight, and it takes time for high-growth companies to achieve their full potential. By focusing on the long-term potential of a company rather than short-term gains, investors can avoid making rash decisions based on market fluctuations.

Finally, it is essential to stay informed and educated about the companies in which you invest. This involves keeping up-to-date with industry trends, market dynamics, and the financial health of the companies you hold. By staying informed, you can make better investment decisions and avoid making decisions based on emotions or rumours.

Key takeaways,

Investing in multibagger stocks involves understanding the psychology of investing and managing emotions such as fear and greed.

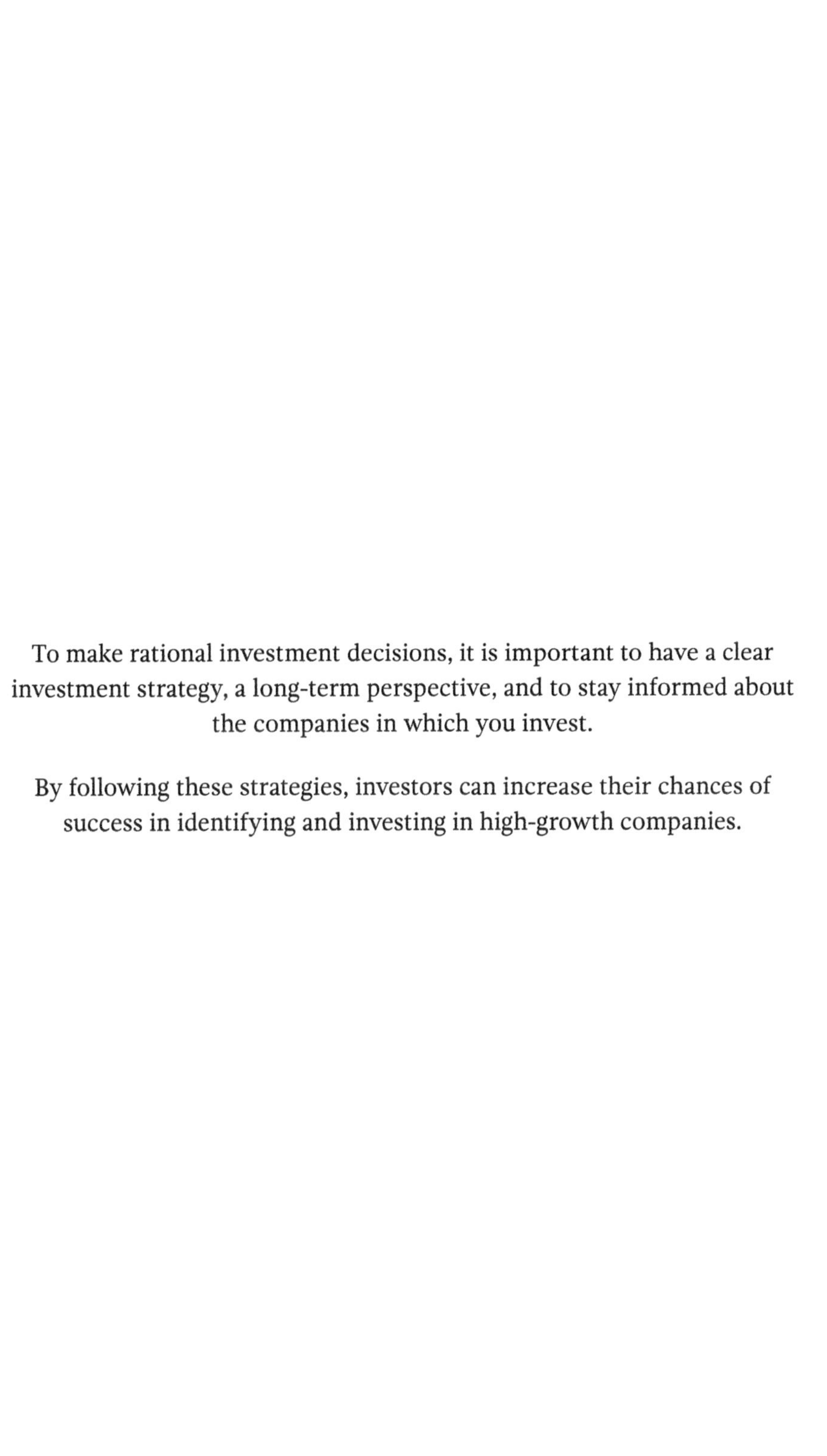

To make rational investment decisions, it is important to have a clear investment strategy, a long-term perspective, and to stay informed about the companies in which you invest.

By following these strategies, investors can increase their chances of success in identifying and investing in high-growth companies.

CHAPTER THREE

Fundamental Analysis: The Foundation of Multibagger Investing

Fundamental analysis is the process of examining a company's financial statements and economic indicators to determine its intrinsic value. In this chapter, we will explore the various aspects of fundamental analysis and how it can be used to identify multibagger stocks.

Fundamental analysis involves examining a company's financial statements, including its balance sheet, income statement, and cash flow statement.

These statements provide a snapshot of the company's financial health and can be used to calculate important financial ratios such as price-to-earnings ratio (P/E ratio), price-to-book ratio (P/B ratio), and earnings per share (EPS).

In addition to financial statements, fundamental analysis also involves examining a company's economic indicators, such as industry trends, market share, and competitive advantages. By analysing these factors, investors can gain insight into a company's long-term growth potential.

One of the key benefits of fundamental analysis is that it provides a long-term perspective on a company's financial health. By focusing on factors such as revenue growth, profit margins, and return on equity (ROE), investors can identify companies with a strong financial performance and the potential to generate high returns. These companies are often referred to as multibagger stocks, as they have the potential to deliver exceptional returns over the long-term.

CHAPTER FOUR

Technical Analysis: A Complementary Approach to Multibagger Investing

Investing in multibagger stocks often involves a combination of fundamental analysis and market trends. Technical analysis is another approach that can be used to complement these strategies and improve investment decision-making. In this chapter, we will explore technical analysis and how it can be used as a complementary approach to multibagger investing.

Technical analysis involves studying charts and historical market data to identify trends, patterns, and signals that can be used to predict future market movements. This approach is based on the idea that market trends tend to repeat themselves, and that historical price and volume data can provide insight into future market behaviour.

One of the primary benefits of technical analysis is that it can provide insight into short-term market movements that may not be visible through fundamental analysis. This can be particularly useful for investors who are looking to capitalize on short-term price movements or identify potential buying opportunities.

There are several key concepts that are central to technical analysis, including support and resistance levels, moving averages, and chart patterns. Support and resistance levels are areas where the price of a stock has previously found support or resistance, and are often used to identify potential entry or exit points. Moving averages are used to smooth out price fluctuations and identify trends, while chart patterns can provide insight into potential trend reversals or continuation patterns.

While technical analysis can be a powerful tool for identifying market trends and making investment decisions, it is important to note that it is not fool proof. Like all investment strategies, technical analysis comes with its fair share of risks and limitations. For example, technical analysis cannot account for unexpected events or external factors that may impact market behaviour.

In addition, technical analysis should always be used in conjunction with other investment strategies, such as fundamental analysis and market research. By using a combination of these strategies, investors can improve their overall investment

decision-making and increase their chances of success in identifying and investing in multibagger stocks.

Key takeaways,

Technical analysis is a complementary approach to multibagger investing that can provide valuable insights into market trends and short-term price movements.

While it comes with its fair share of risks and limitations, it can be a powerful tool when used in conjunction with other investment strategies.

By incorporating technical analysis into your investment approach, you can improve your overall investment decision-making and increase your chances of success in identifying and investing in high-growth companies.

CHAPTER FIVE

The Importance of Valuation in Multibagger Investing

Valuation is a critical component of investing in multibagger stocks. While high-growth companies may have significant potential for future growth, they can also be overvalued and prone to market corrections. In this chapter, we will explore the importance of valuation in multibagger investing and provide strategies for incorporating valuation into your investment approach.

Valuation refers to the process of determining the true value of a company or asset. In the context of multibagger investing, valuation is used to determine whether a high-growth company is overvalued or undervalued. Overvalued companies may have inflated stock prices that do not reflect their true potential, while undervalued companies may have significant growth potential that is not reflected in their stock price.

One of the primary challenges of multibagger investing is determining whether a high-growth company is overvalued or undervalued. This requires a careful analysis of the company's financial statements, growth projections, and industry trends, as well as an understanding of market dynamics and investor sentiment.

There are several key valuation metrics that are commonly used in multibagger investing, including **price-to-earnings ratio** (P/E ratio), **price-to-sales ratio** (P/S ratio), and **price-to-book ratio** (P/B ratio). These metrics can be used to compare a company's stock price to its earnings, sales, or book value, respectively. In general, lower P/E, P/S, and P/B ratios are indicative of undervalued companies, while higher ratios may indicate overvalued companies.

In addition to these metrics, investors may also use discounted cash flow (DCF) analysis or other valuation models to determine a company's intrinsic value. DCF analysis involves projecting future cash flows and discounting them back to their present value, providing an estimate of a company's intrinsic value.

Incorporating valuation into your investment approach can help to mitigate risk and increase your chances of success in identifying and investing in multibagger stocks. By analysing a company's financial statements, growth projections, and industry trends, as well as using key valuation metrics and models, you can determine whether a high-growth company is overvalued or undervalued, and make more informed investment decisions.

Key takeaways,

Valuation is a critical component of multibagger investing.

By analysing a company's financial statements, growth projections, and industry trends, as well as using key valuation metrics and models, investors can determine whether a high-growth company is overvalued or undervalued.

By incorporating valuation into your investment approach, you can mitigate risk and increase your chances of success in identifying and investing in high-growth companies

CHAPTER SIX

Top-down and Bottom-up Approaches to Identifying Multibagger Stocks

There are two primary approaches to identifying multibagger stocks: top-down and bottom-up. Both approaches have their advantages and drawbacks, and investors may choose to use one or both methods depending on their investment strategy and goals. In this chapter, we will explore the top-down and bottom-up approaches to identifying multibagger stocks and provide insights into how they can be used together for successful investing.

Top-down investing is an approach that starts with an analysis of the broader market trends and macroeconomic factors, and then narrows down to specific sectors and companies. This approach involves identifying the most promising industries and sectors based on macroeconomic factors such as GDP growth, interest rates, and inflation, and then selecting individual companies within those sectors based on fundamental and technical analysis.

One advantage of top-down investing is that it can help investors identify sectors and industries that are poised for growth, which can be especially valuable for identifying multibagger stocks. By starting with a macroeconomic analysis, investors can gain a better understanding of the market forces driving growth and make more informed investment decisions.

Bottom-up investing, on the other hand, involves analyzing individual companies in detail and selecting investments based on their fundamental and technical characteristics. This approach involves examining a company's financial statements, competitive advantages, management team, and growth potential, among other factors.

One advantage of bottom-up investing is that it allows investors to focus on individual companies rather than being swayed by broader market trends or macroeconomic factors. This can be especially useful for identifying undervalued or underappreciated companies that may have significant growth potential.

Incorporating both top-down and bottom-up approaches into your investment strategy can help you identify the best multibagger stocks. By starting with a macroeconomic analysis and identifying promising sectors and industries, you can narrow down your investment options to companies with the best potential for growth. By then conducting a detailed analysis of individual companies, you can identify the best opportunities for investment within those sectors.

Key takeaways,

There are two primary approaches to identifying multibagger stocks: top-down and bottom-up.

Top-down investing involves starting with a macroeconomic analysis and narrowing down to specific sectors and companies, while bottom-up investing involves analysing individual companies in detail.

Incorporating both approaches into your investment strategy can help you identify the best opportunities for investment and increase your chances of success in identifying and investing in high-growth companies.

CHAPTER SEVEN

Screening for Multibagger Stocks: Quantitative and Qualitative Factors to Consider

When screening for multibagger stocks, it's important to consider a range of quantitative and qualitative factors. Quantitative factors include metrics such as earnings growth, revenue growth, and return on equity, while qualitative factors include factors such as market positioning, competitive advantages, and management team quality. In this chapter, we will explore the quantitative and qualitative factors to consider when screening for multibagger stocks.

Quantitative Factors

Quantitative factors are objective metrics that can be measured using financial statements and other data sources. These metrics can provide insight into a company's financial health, growth potential, and valuation. Some of the key quantitative factors to consider when screening for multibagger stocks include:

1. Earnings growth: Look for companies with consistent earnings growth over time, as this can be a sign of a company's strong competitive position and ability to generate profits.

1. Revenue growth: Companies with high revenue growth rates may have strong potential for future growth, especially if they are in a growing market.

3. Return on equity (ROE): ROE measures the amount of net income returned as a percentage of shareholders' equity. High ROE can be a sign of a company's efficiency in generating profits.

4. Price-to-earnings (P/E) ratio: The P/E ratio is the ratio of a company's stock price to its earnings per share. Lower P/E ratios may indicate undervalued companies with strong growth potential.

5. Price-to-sales (P/S) ratio: The P/S ratio is the ratio of a company's stock price to its revenue per share. Lower P/S ratios may indicate undervalued companies with strong growth potential.

Qualitative Factors

Qualitative factors are subjective and harder to measure, but can provide valuable insights into a company's potential for growth and success. Some of the key qualitative factors to consider when screening for multibagger stocks include:

1. Market positioning: Look for companies with a strong competitive position in their market, as this can be a sign of long-term growth potential.

1. Competitive advantages: Companies with unique products, technologies, or intellectual property may have a competitive advantage over their peers, making them more likely to succeed over the long term.

3. Management team quality: Look for companies with experienced and capable management teams, as this can be a sign of effective leadership and sound decision-making.

4. Industry trends: Consider the broader industry trends and market dynamics that may impact a company's growth potential.

5. Growth potential: Consider a company's potential for growth based on its product pipeline, expansion plans, and other factors that may impact its long-term prospects.

Incorporating both quantitative and qualitative factors into your screening process can help you identify the best multibagger stocks. By considering a range of factors that impact a company's growth potential and valuation, you can increase your chances of success in identifying and investing in high-growth companies.

Key takeaways,

When screening for multibagger stocks, it's important to consider both quantitative and qualitative factors.

Quantitative factors such as earnings growth, revenue growth, and valuation metrics can provide insight into a company's financial health and growth potential.

Qualitative factors such as market positioning, competitive advantages, and management team quality can provide valuable insights into a company's potential for long-term success.

By incorporating both quantitative and qualitative factors into your screening process, you can increase your chances of success in identifying and investing in high-growth companies

CHAPTER EIGHT

Chapter 8. Analysing Industry Trends and Market Dynamics to Find Multibagger Stocks

Analysing industry trends and market dynamics is a crucial aspect of finding multibagger stocks. While a company may have strong financials and management, the industry it operates in and broader market conditions can have a significant impact on its growth potential and long-term success. In this chapter, we will explore how to analyse industry trends and market dynamics to find multibagger stocks.

Understanding Industry Trends

One of the first steps in analysing industry trends is to identify the key drivers of growth and disruption within the industry. This could include factors such as technological advancements, changes in consumer behaviour, or shifts in regulatory policies. By understanding the underlying trends that are shaping the industry, you can identify companies that are well-positioned to benefit from these trends.

For example, if you were analysing the healthcare industry, you may identify trends such as an aging population, increasing prevalence of chronic diseases, and advancements in medical technology. Companies that are developing innovative treatments for chronic diseases or leveraging technology to improve healthcare delivery could be well-positioned for growth within this industry.

Assessing Market Dynamics

In addition to analysing industry trends, it's also important to assess the competitive landscape and market dynamics within the industry. This could include factors such as the market share of key players, the level of competition within the industry, and the potential for new entrants to disrupt the market.

When assessing market dynamics, it's important to consider the potential risks and opportunities for each company. For example, a company with a dominant market share may be at risk of losing market share to new entrants or disruptive technologies. On the other hand, a company with a unique product or service may have a competitive advantage that can help it maintain or grow its market share over time.

Applying Industry Analysis to Multibagger Investing

By analysing industry trends and market dynamics, you can identify companies that are well-positioned for long-term growth and success. Companies that are operating in industries with favourable trends and market dynamics, and that have competitive advantages or unique products, are more likely to become multibagger stocks.

When analysing industry trends, it's important to consider both short-term and long-term trends. While a company may be well-positioned to benefit from short-term trends, such as an uptick in consumer demand for a particular product or service, it's also important to consider whether the company has a sustainable competitive advantage that can help it succeed over the long term.

In addition to industry analysis, it's important to incorporate other factors such as financial performance, management quality, and valuation into your investment analysis. By taking a holistic approach to investing, you can identify the best multibagger stocks and build a portfolio that is well-positioned for long-term success.

Key takeaways,

Analysing industry trends and market dynamics is a crucial aspect of finding multibagger stocks.

By understanding the underlying trends and competitive landscape within an industry, you can identify companies that are well-positioned for long-term growth and success.

Incorporating industry analysis into your investment analysis can help you identify the best multibagger stocks and build a portfolio that is well-positioned for long-term success.

CHAPTER NINE

Identifying Multibagger Stocks in Emerging Markets

Identifying multibagger stocks in emerging markets can be challenging, but it can also present significant opportunities for growth and investment returns. In this chapter, we will explore how to identify multibagger stocks in emerging markets.

Understanding Emerging Markets

Emerging markets are countries that are experiencing rapid economic growth and development. These markets are typically characterized by lower levels of economic development, higher levels of political risk, and greater potential for growth and volatility than developed markets. Emerging markets include countries such as China, India, Brazil, and many others.

Identifying Multibagger Stocks in Emerging Markets

One of the first steps in identifying multibagger stocks in emerging markets is to identify industries that are likely to experience strong growth in these markets. This could include industries such as healthcare, technology, and consumer goods, which are likely to benefit from rising incomes and changing consumer preferences in emerging markets.

Once you have identified industries with strong growth potential, you can begin to screen for companies that are well-positioned to benefit from these trends. This could include companies with strong brand recognition, innovative products, and competitive advantages that enable them to succeed in these markets.

Another important factor to consider when identifying multibagger stocks in emerging markets is the quality of management. Companies with strong management teams that have a track record of success are more likely to be able to navigate the unique challenges and risks associated with emerging markets.

In addition to analysing individual companies, it's also important to consider the broader economic and political environment in emerging markets. Factors such as currency risk, political instability, and regulatory risk can have a significant impact on the success of companies operating in these markets.

Risks and Opportunities

While there are significant opportunities for growth and investment returns in emerging markets, there are also significant risks that must be considered. These risks include currency fluctuations, political instability, and regulatory risk, among others.

It's important to approach investing in emerging markets with a long-term perspective and to maintain a diversified portfolio to mitigate risk. By investing in a range of companies and industries, you can reduce your exposure to individual company and market risks and increase your chances of identifying multibagger stocks that can deliver significant returns over the long term.

Key takeaways,

Identifying multibagger stocks in emerging markets can be challenging, but it can also present significant opportunities for growth and investment returns.

By identifying industries with strong growth potential and companies with competitive advantages and strong management teams, you can increase your chances of identifying multibagger stocks in emerging markets.

However, it's important to approach investing in emerging markets with a long-term perspective and to maintain a diversified portfolio to mitigate risk.

CHAPTER TEN

Investing in Multibagger Stocks: Key Strategies for Long-term Success

Investing in multibagger stocks can be a lucrative strategy for long-term success. In this chapter, we will explore key strategies that can help investors identify and invest in multibagger stocks for long-term success.

Strategy 1: Identify Companies with Strong Fundamentals

One key strategy for investing in multibagger stocks is to identify companies with strong fundamentals. This includes companies with strong financials, solid management teams, and a track record of delivering consistent growth. By investing in companies with strong fundamentals, investors can increase their chances of identifying stocks that have the potential to deliver significant returns over the long term.

Strategy 2: Focus on Growth Industries

Another key strategy for investing in multibagger stocks is to focus on growth industries. This includes industries such as technology, healthcare, and consumer goods that are likely to experience strong growth in the future. By investing in companies operating in growth industries, investors can increase their chances of identifying stocks that have the potential to deliver significant returns over the long term.

Strategy 3: Conduct Thorough Research

Conducting thorough research is a critical strategy for investing in multibagger stocks. This includes analysing financial statements, industry trends, and competitive landscapes. By conducting thorough research, investors can identify stocks that are undervalued or overlooked by the market, which can provide significant opportunities for long-term growth.

Strategy 4: Diversify Your Portfolio

Diversifying your portfolio is another important strategy for investing in multibagger stocks. By investing in a range of stocks across different industries and geographies, investors can reduce their exposure to individual company and market risks. This can help to protect their portfolio and increase their chances of identifying multibagger stocks that can deliver significant returns over the long term.

Strategy 5: Have a Long-term Perspective

Having a long-term perspective is critical for investing in multibagger stocks. While some stocks may experience short-term volatility or setbacks, it's important to focus on the long-term potential for growth and returns. By having a long-term perspective, investors can stay committed to their investment strategy and avoid making impulsive decisions based on short-term market fluctuations.

Key takeaways,

Investing in multibagger stocks can be a highly rewarding strategy for long-term success.

By focusing on companies with strong fundamentals, growth industries, conducting thorough research, diversifying your portfolio, and having a long-term perspective, investors can increase their chances of identifying multibagger stocks that can deliver significant returns over time.

However, it's important to remember that investing in stocks carries risks and it's important to consult with a financial advisor before making any investment decisions.

CHAPTER ELEVEN

Diversification and Portfolio Management in Multibagger Investing

Diversification and portfolio management are critical components of multibagger investing. In this chapter, we will explore the importance of diversification and portfolio management when investing in multibagger stocks.

Diversification

Diversification is the practice of investing in a range of different assets to reduce the overall risk of an investment portfolio. When investing in multibagger stocks, diversification is critical to mitigate the risks associated with investing in individual stocks. By diversifying your portfolio, you can reduce your exposure to any single stock or industry, which can help to protect your portfolio in case of any downturns in the market.

There are several ways to diversify your portfolio when investing in multibagger stocks. One approach is to invest in stocks across different industries and geographies. This can help to reduce the impact of any individual industry or country-specific risks on your portfolio. Additionally, investing in a mix of large-cap, mid-cap, and small-cap stocks can also help to diversify your portfolio and reduce risk.

Portfolio Management

Portfolio management is the practice of actively managing your investment portfolio to ensure that it aligns with your investment goals and risk tolerance. When investing in multibagger stocks, portfolio management is critical to ensure that your portfolio remains diversified and aligned with your investment objectives.

One key component of portfolio management when investing in multibagger stocks is monitoring the performance of individual stocks in your portfolio.

This includes monitoring the financial performance of each stock, as well as any changes in the competitive landscape or industry trends that may impact the stock's performance.

By actively monitoring individual stocks in your portfolio, you can identify any stocks that may no longer align with your investment objectives and make necessary adjustments.

Another key component of portfolio management is rebalancing your portfolio periodically. Rebalancing involves adjusting the allocation of your investments to ensure that your portfolio remains aligned with your investment objectives and risk tolerance.

For example, if the performance of a particular stock or industry has increased significantly, you may need to rebalance your portfolio to reduce your exposure to that stock or industry and maintain diversification.

Key takeaways,

Diversification and portfolio management are critical components of multibagger investing.

By diversifying your portfolio and actively managing your investments, you can mitigate the risks associated with investing in individual stocks and increase your chances of achieving long-term success.

However, it's important to remember that investing in stocks carries risks, and it's important to consult with a financial advisor before making any investment decisions.

CHAPTER TWELVE

Common Mistakes to Avoid When Investing in Multibagger Stocks

Investing in multibagger stocks can be a rewarding experience, but it also comes with its fair share of risks. In this chapter, we will explore some common mistakes that investors make when investing in high-growth stocks and provide strategies for avoiding them.

Chasing Hype:

One of the most common mistakes that investors make is chasing hype or trends. This involves investing in a stock simply because it is popular or has received a lot of media attention. While it can be tempting to invest in the next big thing, this approach can be risky as it often leads to overvalued stocks that do not deliver long-term growth.

To avoid this mistake, it is essential to do your own research and analysis on the companies in which you are considering investing. This involves looking beyond the hype and examining the company's financials, industry trends, and competitive landscape.

Lack of Diversification:

Another common mistake that investors make is putting all their eggs in one basket. This involves investing too heavily in one stock or sector, leaving investors vulnerable to market volatility and potential losses.

To avoid this mistake, it is important to diversify your portfolio by investing in a range of companies across different sectors and industries. This can help to mitigate risk and provide more stable long-term growth.

Ignoring Valuation:

Investing in multibagger stocks requires a careful balance of growth potential and valuation. Many investors make the mistake of ignoring valuation and investing in high-growth stocks at any price, leading to overvalued stocks that are prone to market corrections.

To avoid this mistake, it is essential to consider the company's valuation and growth potential when making investment decisions. This involves analysing financial statements, growth projections, and industry trends to determine whether a company is overvalued or undervalued.

Not Staying Informed:

Investing in multibagger stocks requires a commitment to staying informed and up-to-date on industry trends and market dynamics. Many investors make the mistake of not staying informed and missing out on key developments that could impact their investments.

To avoid this mistake, it is important to stay informed by reading news articles, analyst reports, and financial statements. This can help you to make better investment decisions and avoid making decisions based on rumours or incomplete information.

Key takeaways,

Investing in multibagger stocks requires a careful balance of risk and reward.

To avoid common mistakes, it is essential to do your own research, diversify your portfolio, consider valuation and growth potential, and stay informed about industry trends and market dynamics.

By following these strategies, investors can increase their chances of success in identifying and investing in high-growth companies.

CHAPTER THIRTEEN

Staying Ahead of the Curve: Monitoring and Reviewing Your Multibagger Stocks

Investing in multibagger stocks requires a lot of effort, research, and monitoring. Even if you have done your due diligence before investing in a stock, it's important to stay ahead of the curve and regularly monitor your investments to ensure that they continue to perform well. In this chapter, we will discuss some key strategies for monitoring and reviewing your multibagger stocks.

Reviewing Financial Statements

One of the most important ways to monitor the performance of your multibagger stocks is by reviewing their financial statements regularly. This includes analysing revenue growth, profitability, and cash flow. If you notice any concerning trends, it may be time to reassess your investment.

Tracking Industry Trends

Another important aspect of monitoring your multibagger stocks is tracking industry trends. Keeping up with the latest developments in the industry can help you identify opportunities and challenges that may impact your investments. This includes tracking regulatory changes, new technology, and competitive pressures.

Paying Attention to News and Events

Monitoring news and events related to your multibagger stocks can also help you stay ahead of the curve. This includes keeping up with earnings releases, management changes, and other news that may impact the company's performance. This information can help you make informed decisions about when to buy or sell your investments.

Setting Realistic Expectations

It's important to set realistic expectations for your multibagger stocks and to regularly review and adjust them as needed. This includes setting target prices for selling your investments and regularly reassessing your investment thesis. By doing so, you can avoid holding onto investments that are no longer meeting your expectations.

Rebalancing Your Portfolio

Finally, it's important to regularly rebalance your portfolio to ensure that it remains diversified and aligned with your investment goals. This involves selling stocks that are overperforming and reinvesting in other opportunities that may have more growth potential.

Key takeaways,

Monitoring and reviewing your multibagger stocks is an ongoing process that requires a lot of effort and attention.

By reviewing financial statements, tracking industry trends, paying attention to news and events, setting realistic expectations, and rebalancing your portfolio, you can stay ahead of the curve and maximize your investment returns.

Remember, investing in multibagger stocks is a long-term strategy, and success requires patience, discipline, and a commitment to ongoing learning and improvement.

CHAPTER FOURTEEN

Selling Multibagger Stocks: Knowing When to Take Profits and Cut Losses

As an investor in multibagger stocks, one of the most challenging decisions you'll have to make is when to sell your investments. Knowing when to take profits and cut losses is crucial to maximizing your returns and minimizing your risks. In this chapter, we'll discuss some key strategies for selling multibagger stocks.

Setting Target Prices

One strategy for selling multibagger stocks is to set target prices for each investment. This involves setting a price at which you will sell the stock, regardless of the reason. This strategy can help you avoid the temptation to hold onto stocks for too long, which can lead to missed opportunities or losses.

Reviewing Financial Statements

Another key factor to consider when selling multibagger stocks is the company's financial performance. If the company's financial statements show signs of declining revenue, declining profitability, or other negative trends, it may be time to sell your investment. Reviewing financial statements regularly can help you identify these trends early on and take action accordingly.

Analysing Industry Trends

Monitoring industry trends is also important when deciding whether to sell a multibagger stock. If the industry is experiencing a downturn or if there are new competitors entering the market, it may be a sign that it's time to sell your investment. Keeping up with industry news and trends can help you identify these signals and make informed decisions.

Paying Attention to News and Events

In addition to industry trends, paying attention to news and events related to the company can also help you decide whether to sell your multibagger stock. This includes news about management changes, lawsuits, and other events that may impact the company's performance. If there are significant negative developments, it may be time to sell your investment.

Cutting Your Losses

Sometimes, even the best investment decisions don't work out. In these cases, it's important to cut your losses and move on. This means selling your investment at a loss before it continues to decline further. While it may be painful to accept a loss, it's better to take action early on rather than hold onto a losing investment.

Key takeaways,

Selling multibagger stocks is never an easy decision, but it's crucial to maximizing your returns and minimizing your risks.

By setting target prices, reviewing financial statements, analysing industry trends, paying attention to news and events, and cutting your losses, when necessary, you can make informed decisions about when to sell your investments.

Remember, investing in multibagger stocks requires patience, discipline, and a long-term perspective, but by staying vigilant and taking action when needed, you can achieve your investment goals.

CHAPTER FIFTEEN

Case Studies of Successful Multibagger Investments

Learning from real-life examples is an excellent way to gain insights into successful multibagger investments. In this chapter, we'll take a look at some case studies of companies that have achieved significant growth and delivered exceptional returns to investors.

Amazon.com

Amazon.com is one of the most well-known examples of a multibagger investment. In the late 1990s, Amazon was a relatively unknown online bookstore that was struggling to turn a profit. However, the company's CEO, Jeff Bezos, had a long-term vision for the company and continued to invest in growth despite the short-term losses.

Over time, Amazon expanded into new markets and product categories, including music, electronics, and clothing. The company also invested heavily in building out its logistics infrastructure and developing new technologies like Amazon Web Services. Today, Amazon is one of the world's largest retailers and has delivered enormous returns to long-term investors.

Microsoft

Microsoft is another well-known example of a successful multibagger investment. In the 1980s and 1990s, Microsoft was a fast-growing software company that dominated the market for PC operating systems. The company's success was driven by its innovative products and its ability to outmanoeuvre competitors like IBM and Apple.

Over time, Microsoft continued to innovate and expand into new markets, including gaming, mobile devices, and cloud computing. The company's stock price has grown by over 60,000% since its IPO in 1986, delivering enormous returns to long-term investors.

Netflix

Netflix is a more recent example of a successful multibagger investment. In the early 2000s, Netflix was a DVD-by-mail rental service that was facing increasing competition from Blockbuster and other traditional video rental stores. However, the company's management team saw an opportunity to disrupt the market by offering a streaming video service.

Over time, Netflix invested heavily in building out its streaming infrastructure and developing original content. Today, Netflix is one of the world's largest streaming video services, with over 200 million subscribers worldwide. The company's stock price has grown by over 15,000% since its IPO in 2002, delivering significant returns to long-term investors.

Key takeaways,

These case studies demonstrate the potential for significant returns from investing in multibagger stocks.

However, they also highlight the importance of long-term thinking, patience, and discipline. Each of these companies faced significant challenges and uncertainties along the way, but their management teams remained focused on their long-term vision and continued to invest in growth.

By learning from these examples and applying the principles of successful multibagger investing, you too can achieve significant returns over the long term.

Printed by Libri Plureos GmbH in Hamburg,
Germany